Valentine's Day   PLATE 1

PLATE 2   Valentine's Day

test pattern

test pattern

Valentine's Day   PLATE 3

test pattern

test pattern

PLATE 4 Valentine's Day / St. Patrick's Day

St. Patrick's Day   PLATE 5

test pattern

PLATE 6   Easter

test pattern

Easter   PLATE 7

For Mother

PLATE 8 Mother's Day

test pattern

Father's Day / Fourth of July   PLATE 9

test pattern

Grandpa

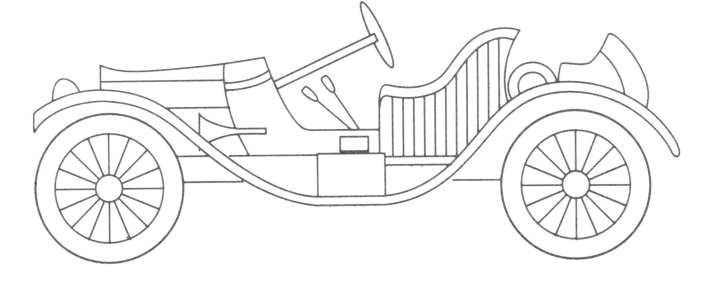

Grandma

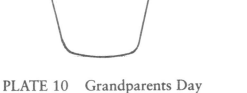

PLATE 10   Grandparents Day

test pattern

PLATE 12   Thanksgiving

test pattern

Kwanzaa   PLATE 13

test pattern

PLATE 14   Christmas

test pattern

Christmas   PLATE 15

test pattern

PLATE 16   Christmas

Peace on Earth

test pattern

test pattern

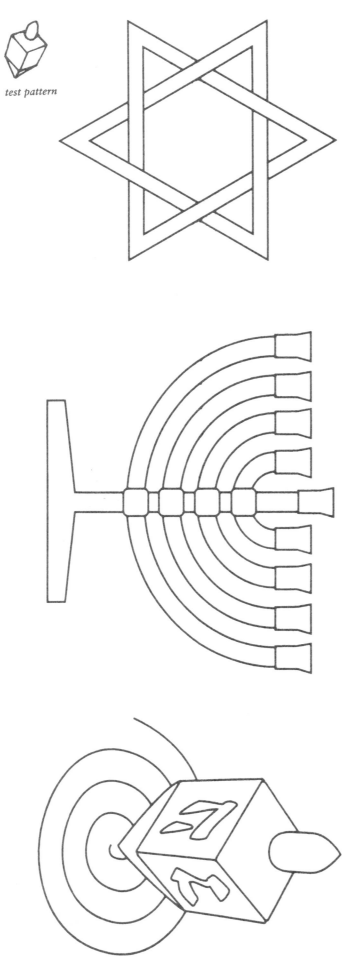

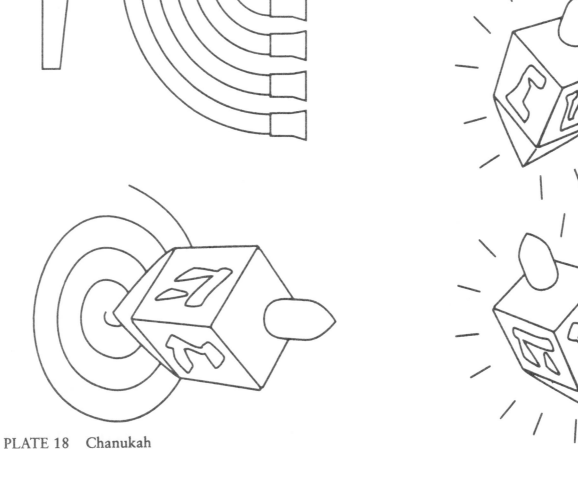

PLATE 18   Chanukah

Happy New Year

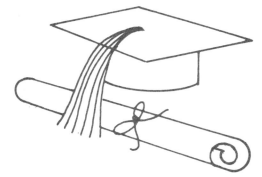

PLATE 20   Graduation

test pattern

Best
Wishes

Wedding   PLATE 21

PLATE 22   New Baby

test pattern

PLATE 24   Birthday / Travel